WHAT ARE YOUR BASIC RIGHTS?

By Jacqueline Laks Gorman
Reading consultant: Susan Nations, M.Ed.,
author/literacy coach/consultant in literacy development

WEEKLY READER®
PUBLISHING

Please visit our web site at www.garethstevens.com
For a free color catalog describing our list of high-quality books,
call 1-800-542-2595 (USA) or 1-800-387-3178 (Canada). Our fax: 1-877-542-2596

Library of Congress Cataloging-in-Publication Data

Gorman, Jacqueline Laks, 1955–
    What are your basic rights? / Jacqueline Laks Gorman.
      p. cm. — (Know your government)
    Includes index.
    ISBN-13: 978-0-8368-8840-9 (lib. bdg.)
    ISBN-10: 0-8368-8840-5 (lib. bdg.)
    ISBN-13: 978-0-8368-8845-4 (softcover)
    ISBN-10: 0-8368-8845-6 (softcover)
    1. Civil rights—United States—Juvenile literature. I. Title.
  KF4749.G67   2008
  342.7308'5—dc   222007038222

This edition first published in 2008 by
Weekly Reader® Books
An Imprint of Gareth Stevens Publishing
1 Reader's Digest Road
Pleasantville, NY 10570-7000 USA

Copyright © 2008 by Gareth Stevens, Inc.

Senior Editor: Brian Fitzgerald
Creative Director: Lisa Donovan
Senior Designer: Keith Plechaty
Layout: Cynthia Malaran
Photo Research: Charlene Pinckney

Photo credits: cover & title page Getty Images/Digital Vision; p. 5 © Dennis Degnan/Corbis; p. 7 Bob Fallcetti/Getty Images; p. 8 Courtesy CNN; p. 9 © Bettmann/Corbis; p. 10 David Schmidt/Masterfile; p. 11 J. Pat Carter/AP; p. 13 © Kim Kulish/Corbis; p. 14 Bob Daemmrich/PhotoEdit; p. 16 Mario Tama/Getty Images; p. 17 Rob Griffith/AP; p. 18 David R. Frazier/PhotoEdit; p. 19 Don Cravens/Time Life Pictures/Getty Images; p. 21 Michael Newman/PhotoEdit

Printed in the United States of America

1 2 3 4 5 6 7 8 9 10 09 08 07

TABLE OF CONTENTS

Words that appear in the glossary are printed in **boldface** type the first time they appear in the text.

CHAPTER 1

The Constitution and the Bill of Rights

In 1787, the United States was a new country. The leaders of the new nation met in Philadelphia, Pennsylvania, to write the **U.S. Constitution.** The Constitution was the plan for the new U.S. government. At first, it did not list the rights, or freedoms, of the people.

Many people wanted the Constitution to be changed. They believed that the Constitution should list the rights of Americans. In 1791, the **Bill of Rights** was added to the Constitution. The Bill of Rights lists many of the freedoms that Americans still have today.

In 1787, the nation's founders met at Independence Hall in Philadelphia to write the Constitution.

CHAPTER 2

The Freedoms of Americans

An **amendment** is a change to the Constitution. The first ten amendments make up the Bill of Rights. These amendments name some of the most important rights held by Americans. People in some other countries do not have these freedoms.

The First Amendment protects freedom of speech. We can say or write what we want. It also gives us the right to meet with others and share our ideas. We can speak with government leaders and ask them to fix problems.

The First Amendment also protects freedom of religion. The government cannot tell people which religion to follow.

Like all Americans, these Muslim men have the freedom to practice their religion.

In some countries, the government controls the news. In the United States, the First Amendment protects freedom of the press. Newspapers, TV stations, and radio stations can print and broadcast the stories they want. They do not have to worry that the government will stop them.

A reporter speaks to a soldier in Iraq. TV stations have the freedom to broadcast the stories they want.

In the 1960s, thousands of people marched for equal rights for African Americans.

Over the years, new amendments have been added to the Constitution. These changes have given more rights to different groups of people. Today, all Americans are equal under the law. No one has more rights than anyone else.

All children in the United States share the right to a free education.

Many of our important rights are not listed in the Constitution. The law protects these rights, too. People have the right to a free education. We have the right to live and work where we choose. All Americans also have the right to **privacy.**

Many people think that the right to vote is the most important right. **Citizens** who are at least eighteen years old can vote in national, state, and local **elections.** By voting, people have a say in how the government is run. Voters choose the leaders they think will do the best job for their community, their state, or the country.

People often wait in long lines to use their right to vote.

CHAPTER 3

Limits on the Government

The people who wrote the Constitution did not want our leaders to be too powerful. The authors put limits on the power of the government. The Bill of Rights protects the rights of the people. The government cannot take away or limit these rights.

After arresting someone, a police officer must tell the person what his or her rights are.

One amendment says that the government cannot search a person's home without a good reason. Other amendments deal with people who are arrested. People who have been arrested must be told what the police think they did wrong. They have the right to a fair public **trial** in a court of law.

A jury helps protect the rights of a person who is on trial. The jury listens to the facts before deciding whether the person broke the law.

People who go to court have the right to a trial by **jury.** A jury is a group of citizens who decide whether the person broke the law. Everyone is believed to be innocent unless the facts show that the person is guilty. If the person is found guilty, the punishment must be fair.

CHAPTER 4

The Responsibilities of Good Citizens

American citizens have many rights. Citizens also have many responsibilities. A responsibility is a duty. We have the responsibility to respect the rights of other people. We also have the duty to protect our rights and the rights of other people.

Tax money pays for firefighters and other workers who help keep us safe.

The biggest responsibility of citizens is to obey the law. Adults must serve on a jury when asked. They also have the responsibility to pay **taxes.** A tax is money paid to the government for important services. Tax money pays our government leaders, teachers, and the police. Tax money also pays for schools and new roads.

Voting is not just a right. It is also an important
responsibility. Voting lets each citizen take part
in the government. People who are eighteen
or older should register, or sign up, to vote. They
should learn about important issues in their country,
state, and town. Then they can make good
decisions when they vote.

Before the 2004 election, voters watched
President George W. Bush talk about important
issues on television.

Good citizens also take an active role in their community. They go to meetings of the city **council** or the school board. Good citizens let their leaders know how they feel about important issues. They try to help solve the problems in their community.

City council meetings give citizens a chance to be heard by their community leaders.

In the 1950s, Rosa Parks (center) fought hard for equal rights for African Americans.

A good citizen can make a big difference in his or her community. In 1955, an African American woman named Rosa Parks helped change history. She was arrested for refusing to give up her seat on a bus to a white man. She inspired people to fight for equal rights. Soon many unfair laws were changed, and people were treated more fairly.

CHAPTER 5

How You Can Be a Good Citizen

You don't have to be old enough to vote to be a good citizen. You can do many things now to help your community.

Being a good citizen means helping other people. You can collect food, clothes, or toys for people in need. You can also help older people in your community by doing chores for them.

People in the United States enjoy many rights. Our freedom depends on people being involved in their government. Our country is at its best when people are active in their community. It's never too early to be a responsible citizen.

Children can be good citizens by cleaning up parks in their city or town.

Glossary

amendment: an official change made to the U.S. Constitution

Bill of Rights: the first ten amendments to the U.S. Constitution

citizen: an official member of a country who has certain rights, such as voting

council: a group of people who are elected to make decisions for a city or town

election: a time when citizens vote for their leaders

jury: a small group of people who decide during a trial whether someone has broken the law

privacy: freedom from having others look into your actions

tax: money that people and businesses pay to the government so that the government can provide important services

trial: the official process of deciding in a court of law whether someone did something wrong

U.S. Constitution: a document that states how the United States is governed

To Find Out More

Books

Becoming a Citizen. A True Book (series). Sarah De Capua (Children's Press)

I Am a Good Citizen. Building Character (series). Mary Elizabeth Salzmann (ABDO Publishing Company)

The Importance of Being an Active Citizen. A Primary Source Library of American Citizenship (series). Anne Beier (Rosen Center Primary Source)

Web Sites

Citizenship
bensguide.gpo.gov/3-5/citizenship/index.html
Learn about the rights and responsibilities that come with citizenship.

How Does Government Affect Me?
pbskids.org/democracy/mygovt/index.html
Find out how important the parts of a community are to everyone.

Publisher's note to educators and parents: Our editors have carefully reviewed these web sites to ensure that they are suitable for children. Many web sites change frequently, however, and we cannot guarantee that a site's future contents will continue to meet our high standards of quality and educational value. Be advised that children should be closely supervised whenever they access the Internet.

Index

About the Author

Jacqueline Laks Gorman grew up in New York City. She attended Barnard College and Columbia University, where she received a master's degree in American history. She has worked on many kinds of books and has written several series for children and young adults. She now lives in DeKalb, Illinois, with her husband, David, and children, Colin and Caitlin. She registered to vote when she turned eighteen and votes in every election.